Living Things and Their Habitats

Welcome to the Rock Pool

by Ruth Owen

Ruby Tuesday Books

Published in 2016 by Ruby Tuesday Books Ltd.

Copyright © 2016 Ruby Tuesday Books Ltd.

Editor: Mark J. Sachner
Designer: Emma Randall
Consultant: Judy Wearing, PhD, BEd
Production: John Lingham

Photo credits
FLPA: 8 (bottom), 10–11, 17 (top), 25, 29 (bottom), 30; Istock Photo: 19 (top); Nature Picture Library: 17 (bottom), 22; Public Domain: 20–21, 30; Science Photo Library: 11 (top right); Shutterstock: Cover, 2–3, 4–5, 6–7, 8–9, 12–13, 14–15, 16, 18, 19 (bottom), 21 (right), 23, 24, 26–27, 28, 29 (top), 30, 31.

British Library Cataloguing in Publication Data (CIP)
is available for this title.

ISBN 978-1-910549-74-2

Printed in India

www.rubytuesdaybooks.com

Contents

Words shown in **bold** in the text are explained in the glossary.

Welcome to the Rock Pool

Who and what lives in a rock pool?

This **habitat** is home to many different types of seaweed.

The residents of this habitat include crabs, starfish and sea anemones.

The living things in a rock pool get what they need to live from their habitat.

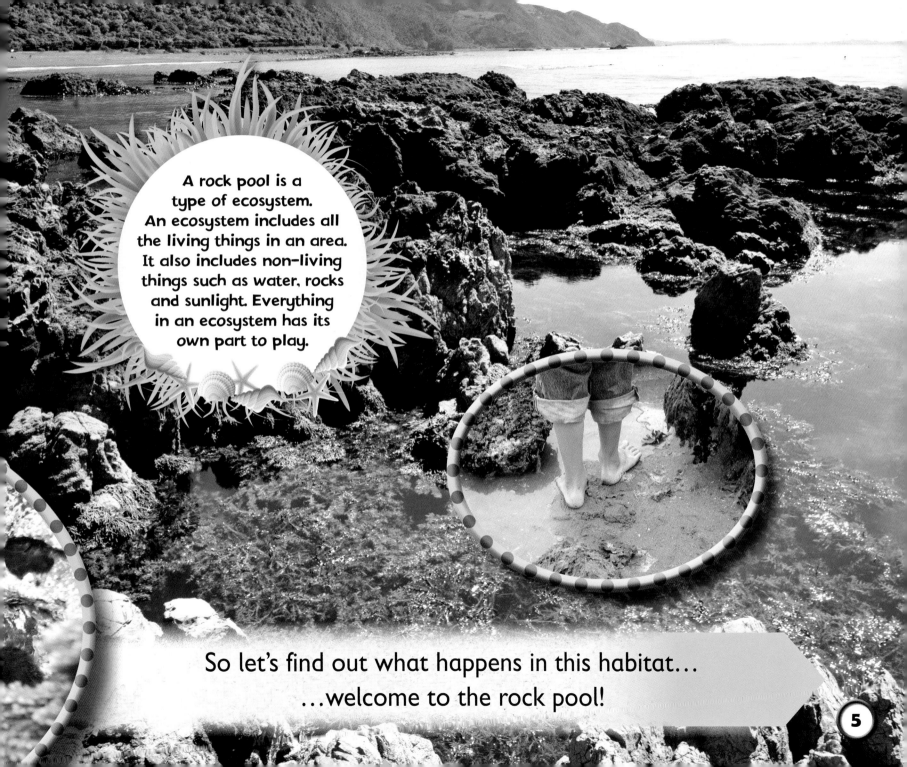

A rock pool is a type of ecosystem. An ecosystem includes all the living things in an area. It also includes non-living things such as water, rocks and sunlight. Everything in an ecosystem has its own part to play.

So let's find out what happens in this habitat...
...welcome to the rock pool!

The Tide Goes Out

At the seashore, waves are crashing against the rocky cliffs.

Then, the **tide** slowly starts to go out, uncovering a beach and craggy rocks.

Rocks

Rock pool

Some seawater gets left behind and forms rock pools between the rocks.

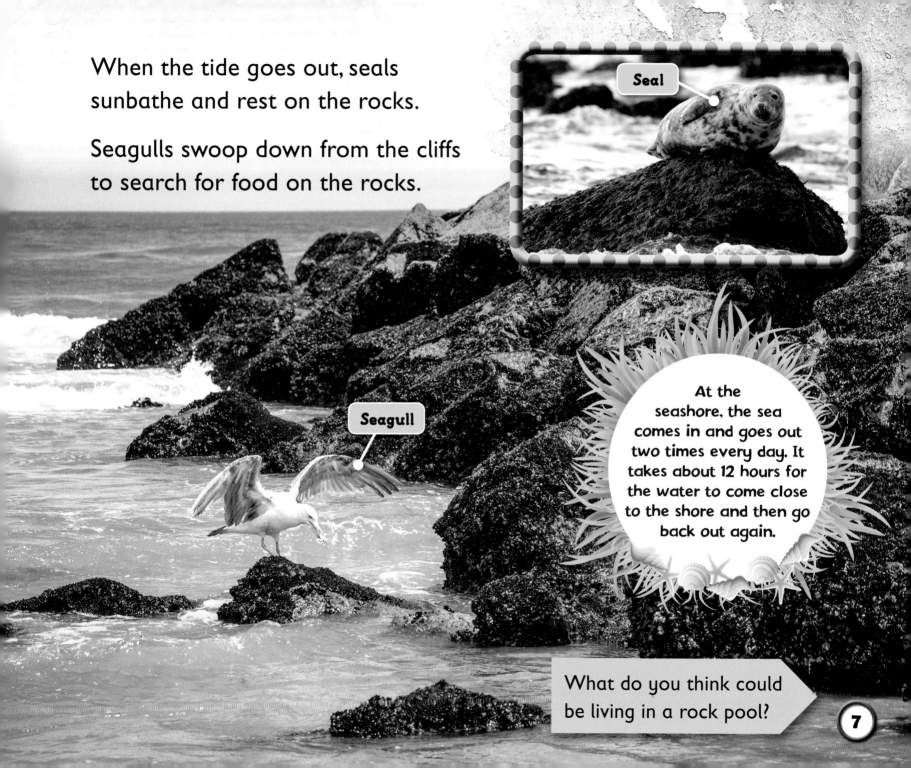

When the tide goes out, seals sunbathe and rest on the rocks.

Seagulls swoop down from the cliffs to search for food on the rocks.

Seal

Seagull

At the seashore, the sea comes in and goes out two times every day. It takes about 12 hours for the water to come close to the shore and then go back out again.

What do you think could be living in a rock pool?

Too Tiny to See!

When you peer into a rock pool, you might spot some seaweed or a crab.

Many of the living things, however, are too tiny to see with your eyes alone.

These **microscopic** rock pool residents are **plankton**.

This photo of plankton was taken with a microscope.

Some of the plankton are plant-like living things called **algae**.

They float in water and use sunlight to make their own food inside themselves.

One litre of rock pool water can be home to 2 million microscopic algae!

Rock pool

Rock pools are also home to zooplankton. What do you think this could be?

Microscopic Animals

A rock pool is home to millions of tiny, floating animals called zooplankton.

Most zooplankton can only be seen with a microscope.

Some of these animals, such as copepods, stay tiny for their whole lives.

A copepod

Zooplankton feed on microscopic algae and on each other. Some zooplankton feed on tiny bits of dead ocean animals.

This photo was taken with a microscope.

This tiny zooplankton creature will grow up to be a shore crab.

A microscopic baby starfish

Some zooplankton are actually the babies of bigger ocean creatures.

Crabs, jellyfish and starfish all start life as floating zooplankton.

What looks like a plant, but is actually a type of algae?

11

All About Seaweed

A rock pool is home to green, red and brown seaweeds.

Most types of seaweed look like plants, but they are actually algae.

Seaweeds cling to rocks or the sandy seabed with a part called a holdfast.

Seaweed

Seaweeds make the food they need for energy inside themselves. To do this, they use sunlight. Some fish, crabs, seabirds and other seashore animals eat seaweed.

When the tide goes out, seaweed becomes a hiding place for crabs and other rock pool animals.

They hide under seaweed from seabirds that try to eat them.

What else do you think is clinging to the rocks in a rock pool?

Clinging to the Rocks

The rocks around a rock pool may have thousands of mussels and limpets clinging to them.

Mussels are soft-bodied animals with blackish-blue shells.

Soft body parts inside shell

A mussel

Two-part shell

When the tide comes in, mussels feed on plankton in the water.

Each limpet has its own spot on a rock that is its home.

It holds onto the rock so tight that it is difficult for birds and other **predators** to remove it!

A limpet's soft body

Shell

A limpet clinging to a rock

Once the tide comes in, a limpet moves around underwater feeding on seaweed. Before the tide goes out again, it returns home. It finds the exact spot on the rocks where it usually lives.

A barnacle is an animal that clings to rocks and doesn't move around. How does it catch its food?

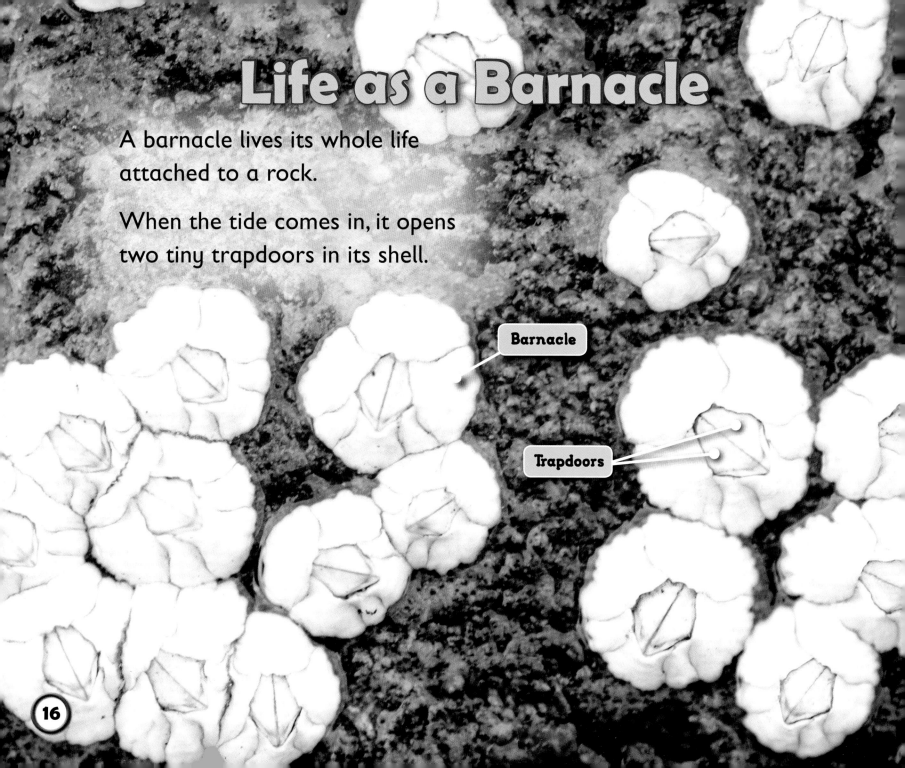

Life as a Barnacle

A barnacle lives its whole life attached to a rock.

When the tide comes in, it opens two tiny trapdoors in its shell.

Barnacle

Trapdoors

The barnacle's 12 legs emerge from the shell.

Then it grabs plankton from the water with its legs.

When the tide goes back out, the barnacle shuts its trapdoors to stay safe from predators.

Microscopic baby barnacles

Legs

When a baby barnacle hatches from its egg, it lives as microscopic plankton. When it's ready to begin its adult life, it attaches to a rock and grows a shell.

What animals look like flowers and stars and munch on their rock pool neighbours?

Hungry Hunters

Sea anemones and starfish are hunters that live in rock pools.

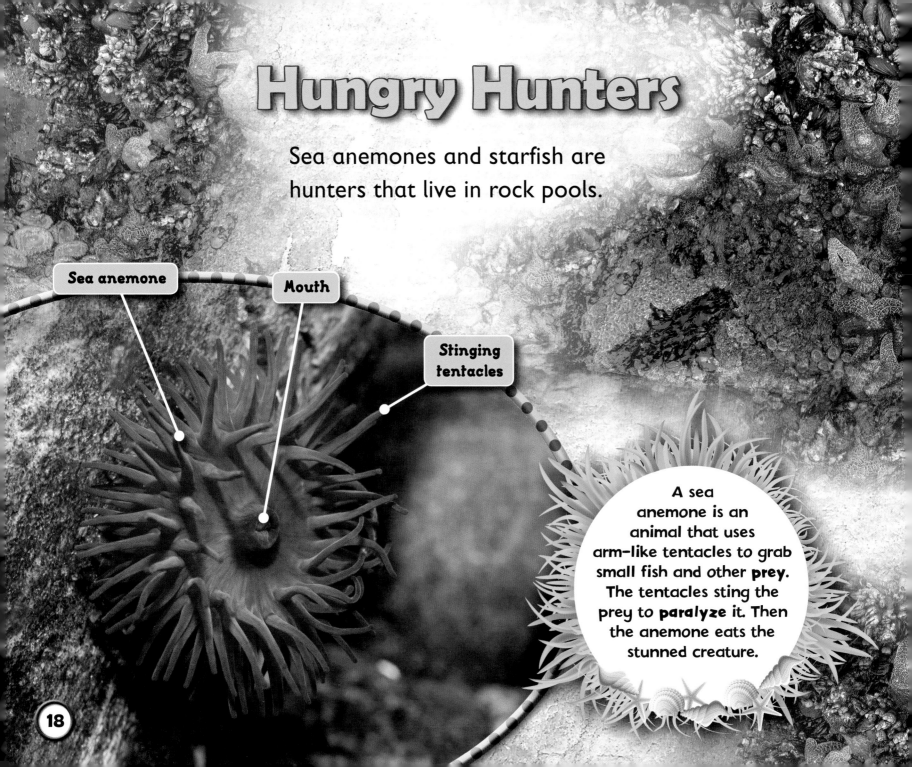

Sea anemone

Mouth

Stinging tentacles

A sea anemone is an animal that uses arm-like tentacles to grab small fish and other **prey**. The tentacles sting the prey to **paralyze** it. Then the anemone eats the stunned creature.

A starfish has caught a mussel.

Using the tiny feet on its underside, it pulls open the mussel's shell.

Then the starfish pushes its own stomach out through its mouth and into the shell.

Juices from the starfish's stomach turn the mussel into a soupy mush.

Then the starfish sucks its stomach and its mushy meal back into its mouth.

Mussel

A starfish's mouth is on its underside.

Tiny feet

Some of these barnacle shells have a hole in the top and are empty. What has happened here?

A Dog Whelk Goes Hunting

A dog whelk is a predatory water snail that feeds on barnacles, limpets and mussels.

The whelk has a hard, rough body part called a radula.

It uses its radula to bore a hole in its prey's shell.

The whelk also produces a chemical that can dissolve the shell.

Once the whelk has broken through the shell, it feeds on its prey's soft body.

Dog whelks

Empty barnacle shells

A dog whelk isn't only a rock pool predator, it's also prey. Crabs and seabirds, such as oystercatchers, feed on dog whelks, mussels, barnacles and limpets.

An oystercatcher

When is a dog whelk not a dog whelk?

When Is a Dog Whelk Not a Dog Whelk?

When it's a hermit crab living in a dog whelk shell!

Dog whelk shell

A hermit crab

A hermit crab has a soft body, but no shell to protect it from predators.

The crab searches its habitat for empty shells that once belonged to its neighbours.

When it finds one that's a perfect fit, it moves in!

As a hermit crab grows, it gets too large for its borrowed shell. So it finds a new, bigger shell and moves in. Its old shell may be useful to a younger, smaller hermit crab.

Why do you think crabs are sometimes known as the rock pool clean-up crew?

23

A Rock Pool Clean-Up Crew

Shore crab

Many types of crabs eat almost anything!

Shore crabs feed on dog whelks, barnacles and other rock pool neighbours.

If a dead fish or other animal washes into the pool, shore crabs eat this, too.

That's why they get the nickname of the clean-up crew.

The hungry shore crabs help keep a rock pool clean.

A female shore crab

A female shore crab lays about 200,000 eggs. She carries the eggs under her body. When the baby crabs hatch, they live as zooplankton until they grow bigger.

Eggs

What other seashore residents help keep the rock pool clean?

Gulls Drop in for Dinner

The seashore is home to herring gulls, or seagulls.

These large birds eat fish, crabs, starfish – anything that lives in a rock pool!

They also feed on dead animals and human rubbish.

A seagull eating a dead fish

Seagulls often fight over food and steal scraps from each other.

A seagull eating a starfish

Mother seagull

Chick

Seagulls build nests of grass and seaweed on rocky cliffs and the roofs of seashore buildings. The parent birds feed their chicks with mushy food from their beaks.

What do you think a seagull does when the tide comes in?

The Tide Comes In

When the tide starts to come back in, waves wash in and out over the rock pools.

Finally, the rock pools disappear underwater.

The residents of a rock pool are changing all the time. As new animals get washed in by the tide, others get washed out.

Seagulls bob up and down on the sea searching for floating snacks.

Under the surface, a fish called a blenny searches for barnacles and crabs to munch on.

The rock pool seaweed floats in the water.

A blenny

For now, the rock pools are part of the ocean.

But soon the tide will turn again....

A Rock Pool Food Web

A food web shows who eats who in a habitat.

This food web diagram shows the connections between some of the living things in a rock pool.

Seaweeds and other algae can make the food they need for energy inside themselves. To do this they need sunlight.

The arrows mean: **eaten by**

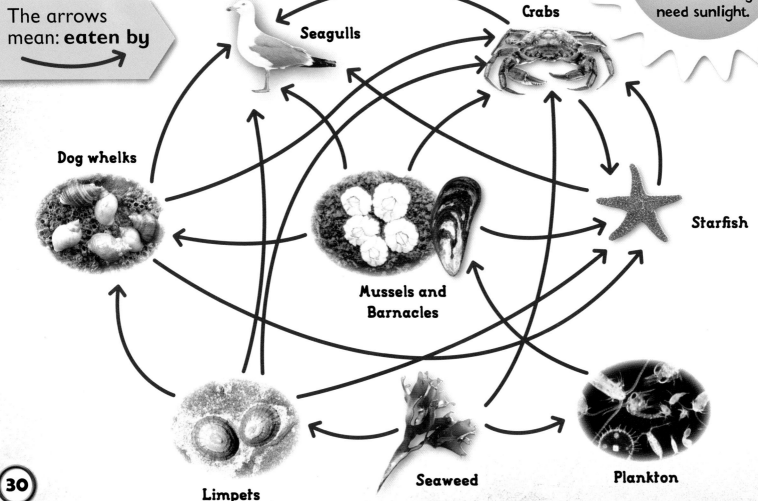

Seagulls

Crabs

Dog whelks

Mussels and Barnacles

Starfish

Limpets

Seaweed

Plankton

Glossary

algae
Plant-like living things that mostly grow and live in water. Like plants, algae can make their own food using sunlight. Seaweed is a type of algae.

habitat
The place where living things, such as animals and plants, live and grow. A rock pool, pond or forest is a type of habitat.

microscopic
Able to be seen only with a microscope, not with the eyes alone.

paralyze
To make an animal or person unable to move.

plankton
Microscopic living things, such as animals and algae, that float in water.

predator
An animal that hunts and eats other animals.

prey
An animal that is hunted by other animals for food.

tide
The rise or fall of the sea that causes the water to come closer to the shore or move farther away. The tide comes in and goes out twice in every 24 hours.

Index

Learn More Online

To learn more about life in a rock pool, go to

www.rubytuesdaybooks.com/habitats